"十一五"期间国家重点图书出版规划项目

中国国家汉办重点规划教材

MONKEY KING CHINESE

美猴王汉语

（少儿）

编者：刘富华　王巍　周芮安

翻译：邵壮

北京语言大学出版社
BEIJING LANGUAGE AND CULTURE
UNIVERSITY PRESS

THE MONKEY KING

Sun Wukong, the Handsome Monkey King, is the hero of the Chinese literary classic *Journey to the West* (Wu Cheng'en, the Ming Dynasty). This novel was based on a true story of a famous Chinese monk, Xuan Zang (602 ~ 664). After years of trials and tribulations, he traveled on foot to what is today India, the birthplace of Buddhism, to seek for the Sutra, the Buddhist holy book. Finally he got the sutras and returned to China, or the Great Tang as was called at that time. He translated the sutras into Chinese, thus making contribution to the development of Buddhism in China.

In this novel, Buddha arranged for a monkey to become the monk's disciple and escort him, to ensure that he makes it to the west to get the sutras. The monkey called Sun Wukong, made the adventurous journey with Tangseng (the master), the other two disciples—Zhubajie (the pig-man) and Shaheshang (the monk), and Bailongma (the horse).

Sun Wukong was born out of a rock and fertilized by the grace of Heaven. In the Water Curtain Cave in the Mountain of Flower and Fruit, he was the King of the monkeys. Being extremely smart and capable, he learned all the magic tricks and kungfu from a Taoist master. He can transform himself into seventy-two different images such as a tree, a bird, a beast of prey or a bug as small as a mosquito so as to sneak into an enemy's belly to fight him or her inside out. Using clouds as a vehicle he can travel 108,000 *li* by a single somersault. The handsome Monkey King excelled in supernatural powers, defied hardships and dangers, and killed monsters. He protected his master Xuan Zang to overcome the eighty-one difficulties in fourteen years of the journey, and finally attained the Buddhist scriptures.

The Monkey King who is omnipotent, brave and winsome, is deeply beloved by Chinese children and adults alike even up till now.

To Teachers

Monkey King Chinese (school-age edition) is a series of elementary Chinese language primers for primary school children from the 1st year to the 3rd year in English-speaking countries. This series of textbooks is divided into three levels according to the year rank. Each level consists of two volumes, A and B. There are altogether six volumes and a total vocabulary of 251 words in the three levels.

Owing to a full understanding on the dispositions and learning habits of primary school pupils aged from seven to ten in English-speaking countries, the editors have chosen topics which appeal to children and at the same time decrease difficulties of the contents to add more fun in the learning process. The aim of this series of textbooks is to give the children a preliminary understanding of the Chinese language through fun games and lay a good foundation for future systematic study.

The style and content arrangement of the textbooks are in accordance with the principle of progressing in an orderly and step-by-step way. Some topics among the three levels may be repeated but their difficulty is increased gradually. Words are the focus of the first level; phrases are the focus of the second level; and sentences the third level. The style and content arrangement of each level are as follows:

Level One: Words are the foundation, supplemented by Pinyin, nursery rhymes, handicrafts, and exercises, among which Pinyin are mainly single finals and tones.

Level Two: Word groups and phrases are the foundation, supplemented by Pinyin, nursery rhymes, handicrafts, and exercises, among which Pinyin are compound spellings of initials and finals.

Level Three: Short sentences are the foundation, supplemented by nursery rhymes, Chinese characters coloring tasks, words and expressions for everyday use, handicrafts, and exercises. Compared with the first two levels, Level Three has some simple Chinese characters, words and expressions for everyday use, and functions as a transition for regular Chinese language education.

Some suggestions to teachers:

1. Teacher leads the reading of words and expressions, sentences, nursery rhymes of each lesson using vocabulary cards, Pinyin cards, and CD.

2. Teacher can give some necessary explanations to the Chinese characters, handicrafts and the exercises. Then allow the children to freely express

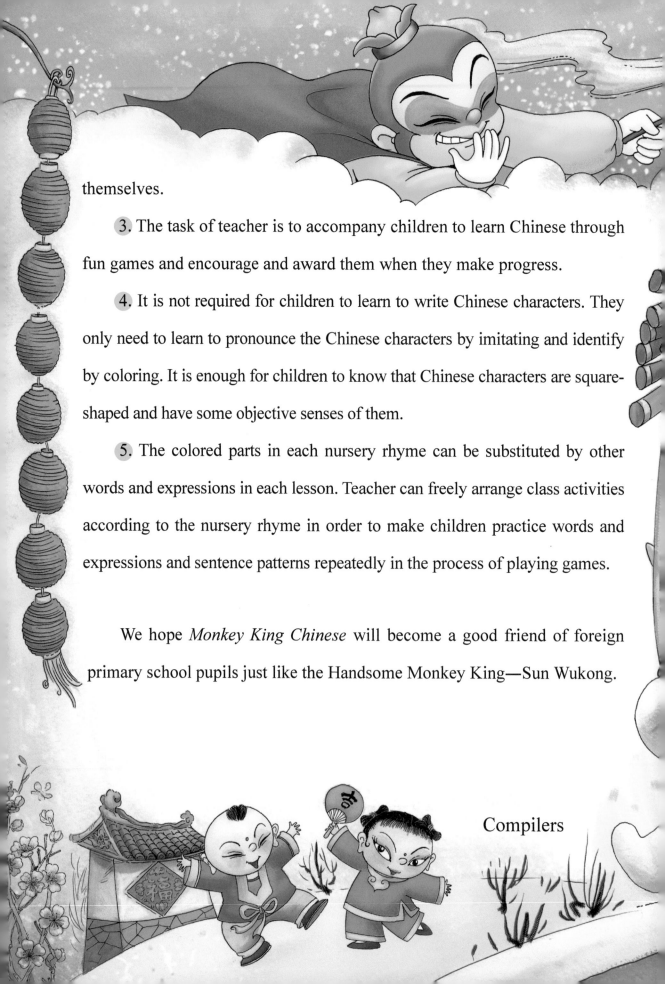

themselves.

3. The task of teacher is to accompany children to learn Chinese through fun games and encourage and award them when they make progress.

4. It is not required for children to learn to write Chinese characters. They only need to learn to pronounce the Chinese characters by imitating and identify by coloring. It is enough for children to know that Chinese characters are square-shaped and have some objective senses of them.

5. The colored parts in each nursery rhyme can be substituted by other words and expressions in each lesson. Teacher can freely arrange class activities according to the nursery rhyme in order to make children practice words and expressions and sentence patterns repeatedly in the process of playing games.

We hope *Monkey King Chinese* will become a good friend of foreign primary school pupils just like the Handsome Monkey King—Sun Wukong.

Compilers

Contents

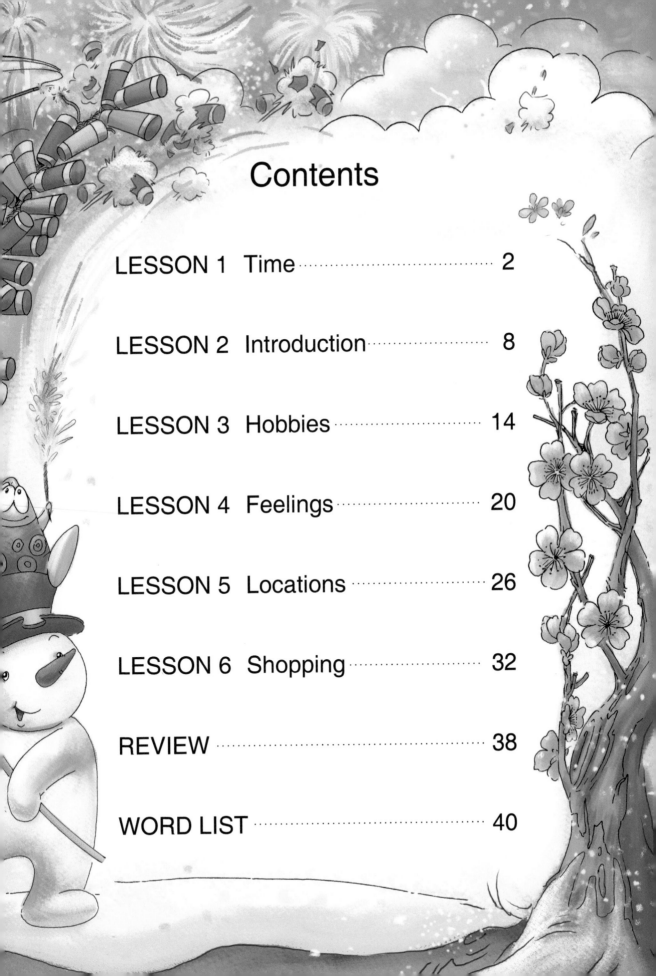

LESSON 1   Time 2

LESSON 2   Introduction 8

LESSON 3   Hobbies 14

LESSON 4   Feelings 20

LESSON 5   Locations 26

LESSON 6   Shopping 32

REVIEW 38

WORD LIST 40

TIME

1. Say it.

Xiànzài   qī   diǎn.
现在 七 点。

zǎoshang
早上

Xiànzài   shí'èr   diǎn.
现在 十二 点。

zhōngwǔ
中午

Xiànzài   jiǔ   diǎn.
现在 九 点。

wǎnshang
晚上

2. Chant it.

Qǐngwèn, qǐngwèn,

Xiànzài jǐ diǎn?

Xiànzài shí diǎn.

Xièxie, zàijiàn.

Excuse me, excuse me,

What time is it?

It is ten o'clock.

Thank you, goodbye.

3. Color it.

 永

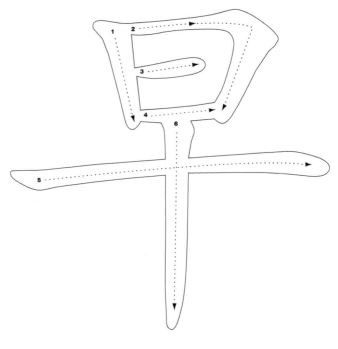

4. Try it.

> Wǒ jiào Dīngdīng.
> 我叫丁丁。

My name is Dingding.

5. Do it.

Paper-cut: snowflakes

Monkey King Chinese 3B

6. Exercises.

(1) Join the dots and match.

wǎnshang

zǎoshang

zhōngwǔ

(2) Stick and read.

sān diǎn
三 点

wǔ diǎn
五 点

shí diǎn
十 点

bā diǎn
八 点

(3) Read and choose 😃 or 🙁.

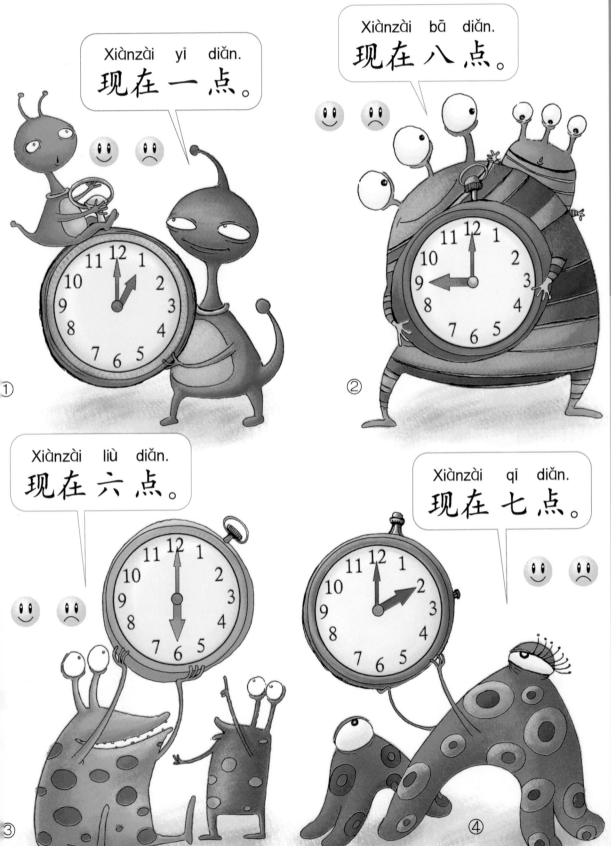

INTRODUCTION

1. Say it.

sījī
司机

lǎoshī
老师

jǐngchá
警察

yóudìyuán
邮递员

chúshī
厨师

Wǒ shì xuésheng.
我是学生。

xuésheng
学生

Wǒ shì ……
我是……   I am...

2. Sing it.

Xiǎo Shǒu Pāi Pāi

小手拍拍

作曲：汤韵

Allegretto

Xiǎo shǒu pāi pāi, xiǎo shǒu pāi pāi,

shǒu zhǐ shēn chu lai.

Chú shī zài nǎ li?

Chú shī zài zhè li.

Chú shī zhēn kě

ài.

Clap your little hands,
Clap your little hands,
And stretch out your fingers.
Where is the cook?
Here it is.
How cute the cook is!

Monkey King Chinese 3B

3. Color it.

 永

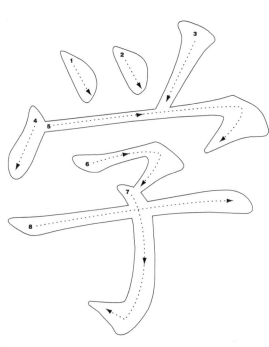

4. Try it.

Wǒ shì xiǎoxuéshēng.
我 是 小学生。

I am a pupil.

5. Do it.

Draw a clown.

Draw the right part of the clown's face according to its left part.

6. Exercises.

(1) Join the dots and match.

lǎoshī   chúshī

jǐngchá   yóudìyuán

(2) Color and read.

Wǒ shì sījī.
我 是 司机。

(3) Listen, number and say.

HOBBIES

1. Say it.

dǎ bàngqiú
打 棒 球

dǎ pīngpāngqiú
打 乒乓 球

dǎ wǎngqiú
打 网 球

dǎ lánqiú
打 篮 球

Wǒ huì huá bīng.
我 会 滑 冰。

yóu yǒng
游 泳

huá bīng
滑 冰

Wǒ huì ……
我 会…… I can...

2. Chant it.

Xiǎoxiǎo yùndòngyuán,

Láidào tǐyùguǎn.

Dǎ bàngqiú, dǎ lánqiú,

Shēntǐ hǎo, cháng duànliàn.

Little sportsman,

Comes to the gym.

Play the baseball, play the basketball.

Do exercises frequently and be in good health.

3. Color it.

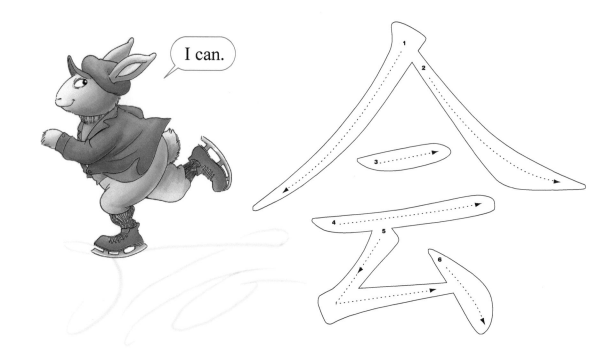

I can.

4. Try it.

Wǒ bā suì.
我八岁。

I am eight.

5. Do it.

Color to find the sportsman.

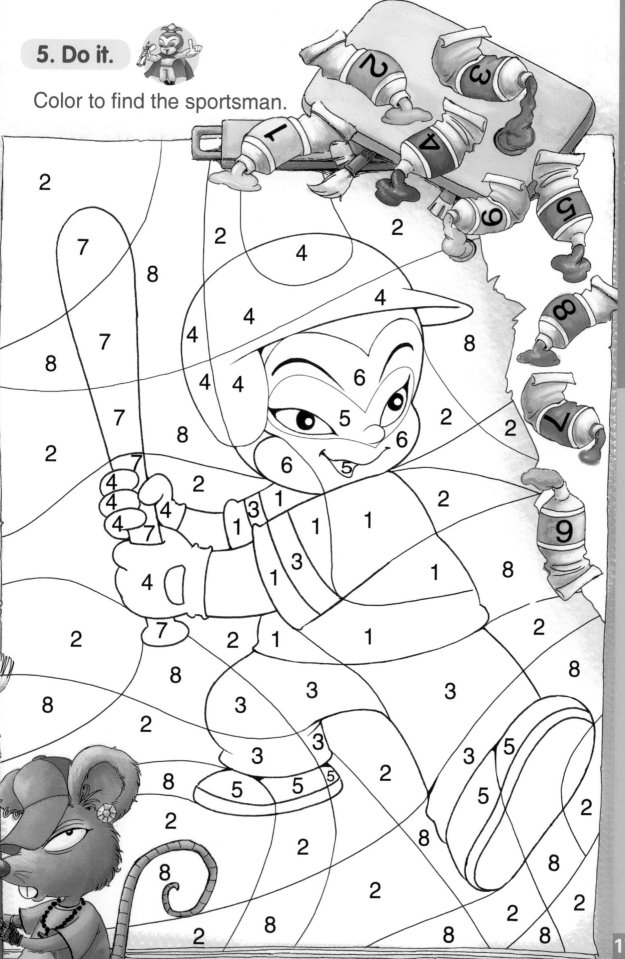

6. Exercises.

(1) Choose the pictures for the two words.

yóu yǒng
游 泳

huá bīng
滑 冰

(2) Match and read.

lánqiú bàngqiú pīngpāngqiú wǎngqiú

(3) Read and choose 🙂 or 🙁.

Wǒ huì yóu yǒng.
我 会 游 泳。

① 🙂 🙁

Wǒ huì dǎ lánqiú.
我 会 打 篮 球。

② 🙂 🙁

Wǒ huì huá bīng.
我 会 滑 冰。

③ 🙂 🙁

Wǒ huì dǎ bàngqiú.
我 会 打 棒 球。

④ 🙂 🙁

FEELINGS

1. Say it.

kě
渴

kùn
困

gāoxìng
高兴

è
饿

nánguò
难过

Wǒ hěn lèi.
我 很 累。

lèi
累

Wǒ hěn……
我 很…… I am very...

2. Sing it.

Xiǎo   Yīngwǔ
小 鹦鹉

作曲：汤韵

Moderato

Xiǎo yīng wǔ,   bù shuō huà.

Zěn me   la?   Zěn me   la?

È   le   ma?   Kě   le   ma?

Bú shì bú shì dōu bú shì.

Wǒ kùn   la,   wǒ kùn   la.

Little parrot keeps quiet.

What is the matter with it?

Is it hungry? Is it thirsty?

No, no, it is none of these.

I am sleepy, I am sleepy.

21

Monkey King Chinese 3B

3. Color it.

4. Try it.

Wǒ   jiā   yǒu   sān   kǒu   rén.
我 家 有 三 口 人。

There are three people in my family.

5. Do it.

Draw facial expressions.

6. Exercises.

(1) Look and draw.

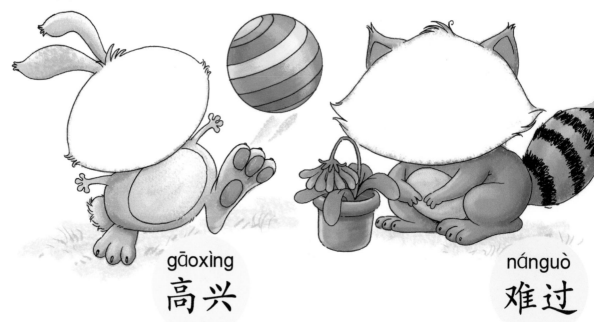

gāoxìng

高兴

nánguò

难过

(2) Listen and number.

(3) Color, write and say.

Wǒ hěn ......

我 很……

Lesson 5

LOCATIONS

1. Say it.

chēzhàn
车站

xuéxiào
学校

huāyuán
花园

yùndòngchǎng
运动场

Wǒ zài gōngyuán.
我在公园。

gōngyuán
公园

...... zài ......
……在…… ...be in/at the...

2. Chant it.

Xiǎopéngyǒu, zhǎo bàba.

Bàba, bàba, zài nǎr ya?

Zài chēzhàn, zài chēzhàn.

Pǎodào chēzhàn qù zhǎo tā.

车站

Little child is looking for father.

Father, father, where are you?

Father is at the bus stop, father is at the bus stop.

So run to the bus stop to look for him.

3. Color it.

4. Try it.

Wǒ xǐhuan gǒu.

我 喜欢狗。

I like dogs.

5. Do it.

Choose Christmas gifts.

Draw your favorite Christmas gifts in Santa Claus' bag and color them.

6. Exercises.

(1) Listen and number.

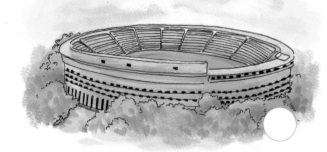

(2) Look and find the Chinese word for garden.

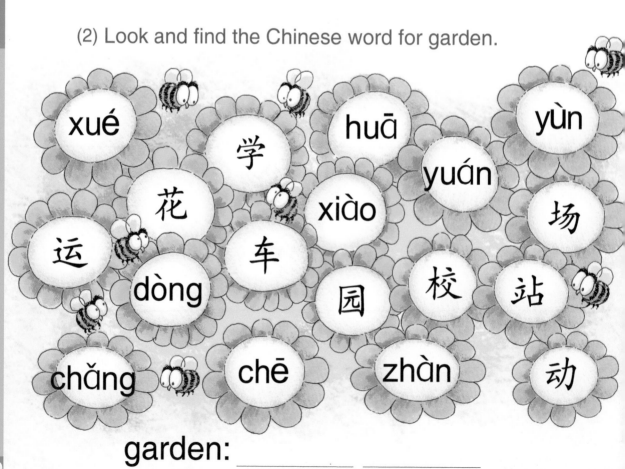

xué 学 huā yùn
花 yuán
运 xiào 场
车 校 站
dòng 园
chǎng chē zhàn 动

garden: _____ _____

(3) Read and match.

Where is mother?

Māma zài chēzhàn.

Māma zài huāyuán.

Māma zài yùndòngchǎng.

Māma zài xuéxiào.

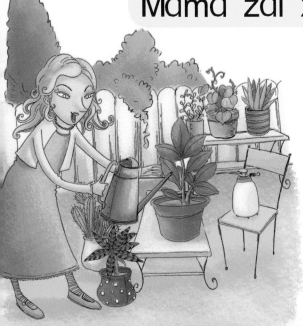

SHOPPING

1. Say it.

bīngjīlíng

冰激凌

tángguǒ

糖果

qiǎokèlì

巧克力

shǔpiàn

薯片

Wǒ mǎi bīngjīlíng.

我买 冰激凌。

bǐnggān

饼干

règǒu

热狗

Wǒ mǎi ......

我买…… I would like to buy...

2. Sing it.

Măi Dōngxi
买东西

Allegretto

作曲：汤韵

Shí pǐn diàn ya dōng xi duō,

yǒu shǔ piànr ya yǒu táng guǒ.

Măi shén me ya măi shén me ya?

Măi shǔ piànr ya gěi gē ge.

The grocery is full of goods.

There are potato chips, there are candies.

What to buy? What to buy?

Buy some potato chips for elder brother.

3. Color it.

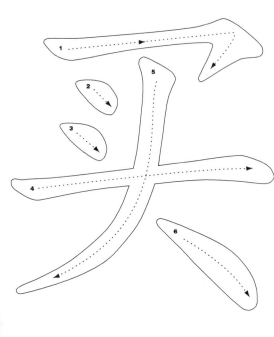

4. Try it.

Wǒ huì shuō Hànyǔ.
我 会 说 汉语。

I can speak Chinese.

5. Do it.

Find the differences.

6. Exercises.

(1) Read and draw 😊 or 🙁.

① **bīngjīlíng**

② **tángguǒ**

③ **règǒu**

④ **bǐnggān**

(2) Tick and read.

	I like it.	I don't like it.
règǒu 热狗		
shǔpiàn 薯片		
qiǎokèlì 巧克力		
bīngjīlíng 冰激凌		

(3) Find, match and answer.

Monkey King Chinese 3B

六点

滑冰

巧克力

警察

打乒乓球

邮递员

糖果

车站

厨师

打棒球

游泳

八点

学生

公园

学校

司机

饼干

十点

打篮球

老师

冰激凌

运动场

花园

热狗

WORD LIST

B

棒球	bàngqiú	baseball	3
冰激凌	bīngjīlíng	ice cream	6
饼干	bǐnggān	biscuit	6

C

| 车站 | chēzhàn | station | 5 |
| 厨师 | chúshī | cook | 2 |

D

| 打 | dǎ | play | 3 |
| 点 | diǎn | o'clock | 1 |

E

| 饿 | è | hungry | 4 |

G

| 高兴 | gāoxìng | happy | 4 |
| 公园 | gōngyuán | park | 5 |

H

| 汉语 | Hànyǔ | Chinese | 6 |

很	hěn	very	4
花园	huāyuán	garden	5
滑冰	huá bīng	skating	3
会	huì	can	3

J

家	jiā	family	4
叫	jiào	named	1
警察	jǐngchá	policeman	2

K

渴	kě	thirsty	4
口	kǒu	(measure word)	4
困	kùn	sleepy	4

L

篮球	lánqiú	basketball	3
老师	lǎoshī	teacher	2
累	lèi	tired	4

M

| 买 | mǎi | buy | 6 |

N

| 难过 | nánguò | sad | 4 |

P

| 乒乓球 | pīngpāngqiú | table tennis | 3 |

Q

| 巧克力 | qiǎokèlì | chocolate | 6 |

R

| 热狗 | règǒu | hot dog | 6 |
| 人 | rén | person | 4 |

S

是	shì	be	2
薯片	shǔpiàn	potato chip	6
说	shuō	speak	6
司机	sījī	driver	2
岁	suì	age	3

T

| 糖果 | tángguǒ | candy | 6 |

W

| 晚上 | wǎnshang | evening | 1 |
| 网球 | wǎngqiú | tennis | 3 |

X

现在	xiànzài	now	1
学生	xuésheng	student	2
学校	xuéxiào	school	5

Y

邮递员	yóudìyuán	postman	2
游泳	yóu yǒng	swimming	3
运动场	yùndòngchǎng	stadium	5

Z

在	zài	at	5
早上	zǎoshang	morning	1
中午	zhōngwǔ	noon	1